CW00349746

Poems

and

Rhymes

for all Times

Natalie Mason

PNEUMA SPRINGS PUBLISHING UK

First Published in 2012 by:
Pneuma Springs Publishing

Poems and Rhymes for all Times
Copyright © 2012   Natalie Mason

Natalie Mason has asserted her right under the Copyright, Designs and Patents Act, 1988, to be identified as Author of this Work

Pneuma Springs

British Library Cataloguing in Publication Data

Mason, Natalie.

Poems and rhymes for all times.

1. Life--Poetry. 2. Manners and customs--Poetry.

I. Title

821.9'2-dc23

ISBN-13: 9781907728426

Pneuma Springs Publishing
A Subsidiary of Pneuma Springs Ltd.
7 Groveherst Road, Dartford Kent, DA1 5JD.
E: admin@pneumasprings.co.uk
W: www.pneumasprings.co.uk

To

Lee & the three special girls in my life, Rebecca, Kayleigh & Jessica

CONTENTS

<u>Poems</u>

Rhymes

Tributes

Poems

Life

Enjoyable, fun and exciting,

Mysterious, exhausting, too much fighting
So many happy times to be had,
Although times may also be sad

Is there a path we are meant to take?
Which direction, what decision to make
Enjoy a moment; wish it could last forever,
The moment big or small, alone or together

Living your life, then something goes wrong,
This isn't what you had planned all along
All of a sudden things get confusing,
It's just a learning curve, one day you will find it amusing

Thing's can happen for a reason, though at the time
unexpected,
It's not the end of the world; just means life has been re-
directed
Didn't know where life was going, or even which way to go?
Sometimes there will be highs, others may be low

Such a busy life, try to stop the hurrying,
Enjoy the time you have with minimal worrying
All our lives are different, just enjoy the mystery
Fulfil it as much as possible, make an exciting history.

Special Birthdays

Your birth being zero is a special age,
It is the beginning of life's first page
Probably the most fuss you will ever get,
Cannot even remember the people you have met
So many parties in-between ages,
Friends, presents, milestones throughout different stages

You reach teenage years, the big thirteen,
Are you nice, or have you turned mean?
Hormones kick in, body starts to change,
All of a sudden you are feeling strange

You arrive at sweet sixteen, getting over mood swings?
Growing up fast, into all new things
Feel grown up; don't want to be treated like a child,
Not old enough to drink but want to go wild!

Eighteen comes after all of that waiting,
Good times to be had, done some dating?
Been through phases, your personality has grown,
This could be the time for a big party to be thrown

Twenty one, a good age to reach for most, so it seems,
Old enough to take charge of yourself, young enough to
accomplish dreams
Years go by until the next big one
Built up your life, as birthdays have come and gone

Time to stand on your own two feet,
Taking new paths, new people to meet
Maybe settled down, got a family at thirty?
Not for you, cannot settle, enjoy being flirty?

The big Forty, slowly drifting out of your youth,
Along your way been through ups and downs, learnt lies and truth
Some people say it's down hill from here,
Embrace and celebrate, or shed a tear?
Know who you are and where you want to be,
After forty years you can finally see

At fifty what wisdom, you are so wise,
At one time you were asking, now you can advise
Been through a lot, have such pride and grace,
Have confidence in life, you are in a good place
All of the way to sixty, you may be a grandparent and
feeling good,
Start to slow things down and look after yourself now
you should

A few aches and pains as eighty creeps up,
Time to wind down, happy with a warm drink in your
cup
Maybe you need glasses for reading,
Find your hair has started receding
Need a hearing aid for television,
A comfy chair in the right position

Make it to one hundred, good for you,
How many generations have you made it through?
Don't want a fuss, don't need anything,
People around you, amazed at such a life you bring
Look back on your life, all you have achieved,
Had a family, built friendships, all the joy you have
received
How many times have you moved house, even moved
away?
Think of all of the jobs you've had, all the different types
of pay!

Penny, farthing, the shilling,
All different types of billing
Technology has changed so much,
Everything is a button or screen to touch

One hundred years, lucky if you reach it,
A grand old age, one hundred candles to be lit!

Character

Each with a different character, a selection of faith, colour
and race,
Can be reflected with up bringing, the way we are
brought up and the place

All with our own personality, some of us quiet, some
loud,
Our individual way, shy, bubbly, modest or proud
Deal with situations, depending on confidence or nerves,
Our character can show if we are happy, if pale, dark,
thin or with curves

Stubborn and selfish, dramatic with greed,
Patient, popular, a party animal who likes to take lead
Easily angered with a temper, likes to take control,
An understanding character, with a kind soul

Some are bullies, have a mean streak,
A character who rebels or attention seek
Our character can change, along with our health,
Can give a new out look, just as can being poor or with
wealth

Love

Love, what a wonderful thing,
The love of family and friends, what a joy it can bring
Parents, a spouse, children or a pet,
We all need love, no matter how much we get

Unconditional love from parents and children, faithful
love from a partner or spouse,
Sentimental love of belongings, material love of things in
your house

Full of love, have the whole package with trust,
Think it is the real thing, or is it just lust?
A small taste of love, even for a short while,
Gives warmth and comfort, helps to make us smile

Showing and giving real love, some can find tough,
Try your best to let it out, you can never give enough
People show love in their own way,
If lucky enough to have it, say it everyday

Wish

Believing in a wish, will it come true?
Wishing hard enough gives hope that is new
It may be in prayer to wish really hard,
Read some wishing words in a special card
Do wishes make you think of fairies, brightness and
butterflies?
Or take you to a different world; a wish may happen by
surprise

Wish it wasn't school or work today,
Wish for money, the bills to go away
Wish for peace and happiness,
Wish your house wasn't in a mess!
Something more serious like your health,
Wouldn't wish for something as small as wealth
Maybe you would wish upon a star,
Pull a wish bone, would you go that far?

What ever your wish, I hope it comes true,
Don't stop trying, wishing is good for you

Memories

So many memories, first ones from childhood,
Snippets of growing up, remember days out that were
good
Do you remember playing with friends, learning to ride a
bike?
Going to family get tog ethers, favourite sweets you'd
like

Maybe certain days stick in your mind, summer days at
the park?
Going to a party, coming home in the dark
First Christmas you remember, the excitement still in
your mind!
Up to mischief, looking for presents you shouldn't ever
find

First time you got your own music, tape, record or C.D?
Listen on an Ipod, moving with technology
Memories with siblings, did you squabble and fight?
Remember the first sleep over that you got an invite?
Staying up, a feast of food until late,
Sat up telling stories all night with your mate
Put together old bed sheets to make a den,
Look back at the simple fun you had back then

A place you were told to be good, your parents made
you go to?
Told to be polite and smile, you were bored the whole
way through!
Unfortunately as well as the good memories, our minds
remember the bad,
Try to hold on to the good ones, and the more good
memories you can add

Trapped

Depression, obsession, your nerves are shot!
Your head is too messed up; you don't know what
you've got!
Trapped inside the wrong body, in so much doubt,
Don't know which way to turn, or what it's all about
Wanting to yell, shout and scream,
Everyday a battle, wish it was a dream
Feel like nobody cares, or understands
Living, time is passing whilst everyone else makes plans
Seconds feel like hours, hours feel like days,
Then time has gone so quickly, feels like a haze

Maybe attracted to the wrong person, someone you
shouldn't,
You tried to hold back, but you just couldn't
What a mess, things would be easier if you could resist,
Looking at the bigger picture now, that is what you
missed!
Getting help, trying to get some answers,
Feel like you are slowly running out of chances

Remember you are worth as much as anyone else,
We are all different, have confidence in yourself.

Phobias and Fears

Phobias and fears we may experience or had in the past,
Some continue for a lifetime, others a short time they last
Phobias can range from spiders, or being scared of
heights,
Or not liking the light off on dark nights
Some phobias are more serious, can control lives
everyday,
Cannot get out of the house, prefer to stay out of the way
Sometimes we cannot control a fear that we feel,
Easy to get over in your mind, in reality is a big deal!

Natalie Mason

Seasons

All year around there are four different seasons,
All can be enjoyable for all different reasons
It starts to get cooler when autumn is here,
Although the sky can still be bright and clear
Leaves off the trees start to fall to the ground,
Rusty brown in colour, they make a crunching sound

Winter creeps in, extra layers we need to wear,
Now all of the branches on trees are completely bare
Dark mornings, dark nights, fog and frost,
A white sheet of snow covers streets as houses get lost
More hot drinks when it is cold, early the curtains are
drawn,
It feels later than it is, the dark makes you want to yawn

Days get longer as forward the clocks go,
Spring is here, everything starts to grow
Trees are filled with blossom, daffodils yellow and bright,
Look all around you, what a pretty sight
Summer is around the corner, grass is green, with
flowers in bloom,
Enjoy the outdoors; the warm season will be here soon
Sun hats and shades, picnics in the park,
Drinks in a beer garden, barbecues until dark

The clocks go back, the nights draw in,
Not long now until autumn will begin
Each one of the four seasons pass us by each year,
If you are not enjoying one of them, you know the next
one is near
However the seasons get mixed up, as you may learn,
Sometimes it will be like winter when it's meant to be
summers turn

18

Inspiration

In many ways we can be inspired,
Ways in which life is handled, can be easily admired
Someone full of personality, strong with motivation?
Follow the path they want in life, work at it without
hesitation

Is there someone who has been given a bad lot?
You are inspired and know you are lucky to have what
you've got
People who live with lost limbs or a wheelchair,
Small things you thought had importance, you now don't
care
Could be inspired by someone critically ill,
They get on with life and show such will

Is there a way of making a difference, deep down you
know you could?
You are filled with inspiration; all of a sudden you know
you should
It may be for a charity, a reminder of something bad,
Somebody's strength to get through a life they once had

Inspired by the way someone carries themselves, with
confidence and pride,
Makes you look at yourself and bring out your best side
Is there someone with the same interests as you?
On television, in music or in a sport you relate to

Take what you can and be inspired,
Follow your heart and you will be admired

Marriage

You know it is time to get married, when you meet your
soul mate,
Look back on your best times, remembering that first
date
The traditional way, the man presents a ring, down on
one knee,
A special moment as he asks to marry his wife to be

The wedding plans start as you choose a date,
Venues and colours for the day you want to create
During the next year or so you continue to plan,
You don't want to be separated from your woman or man

Wedding dress and bridesmaids dresses have finally
been found,
How many shops in total have you had to look around?
Probably more than the groom and his best man,
Usually found their suits in the first shop they began!

It finally arrives; you have been waiting for your big day,
The love you have for each other, with those special
words to say
Then that is it, you will be together, happily married for
years,
During the ceremony emotions run high, with lots of
happy tears

Enjoy each others company, putting up with any niggles,
Being untidy, snoring, none of it matters with love and
giggles
Marriage is about pulling together when times are tough,
It all starts off smooth; you can get through anything if
your love is enough

Pregnancy

Finding out, planned or not?
That test picks up such a small dot!
Starts off so small growing inside,
Cannot believe it's happened, how ever long you've tried
Shock, happiness, emotions and tears,
Excitement, life changing, maybe some fears
First time pregnant or had children before,
It must be great, we keep having more!

Weeks go by and baby starts to grow,
You are noticing a bump is starting to show
Flicking through leaflets and baby books,
Wanting to know each stage, how your baby looks
Described as a pea, orange or pineapple too,
Can't wait for a scan to show him or her inside you
Morning sickness, or have it all day,
Emotional and tired, and then you're okay
So much to think of, what you can and can't eat,
Feeding for two, having a cake as a treat

Do you buy things before baby is born?
Old tales of having things in the house, people do warn
Everywhere you go you are asked how you and baby are,
Have you got a pram, a seat for your car?
Time to get your scan as your pregnancy is moving on,
Finding out if a boy or girl, and if there is just one!
Cannot believe you can see its legs and arms moving around,
Overjoyed as you hear the heartbeat, what an amazing sound
All of this for you to see up on a screen,
You cherish the scan picture to show you have been
Flutters begin feeling like butterflies,

Turning into strong kicks, as your baby changes in size
Almost time, anti-natal classes for baby talk,
Wearing maternity clothes, a slower pace in your walk
Planning the birth, who should you have by your side?
Somebody close to you, to give comfort and guide
Contractions begin, talked about pain relief for you,
A mixture of feelings for what you are about to go
through
Your chosen birth, water, hospital or at home,
The most surreal time in your life on its own!
The pain, panting and screaming during the birth,
You hold your baby in your arms, the most precious
thing on earth

Natalie Mason

New Mother

New mother, am I doing it right?
A new routine from day through to night
You try to settle when you first get home,
Everybody visiting, you are never left alone
The adrenaline rush, how you have done so well,
You have your own birth story to tell
You feel so lucky to have your baby so healthy,
Feel like you have won the lottery, in life you are so
wealthy

Children

Loving, tiring, rewarding, from babies through to walking,
Not babies for long, growing fast, and then they begin talking!
Changing nappies, the sleepless nights,
Feeding with one eye open, no bright lights
Learning on the job, it is a never ending test,
It is the hardest job of all, not always knowing what is best
Working all hours, without any pay,
The only job paid in love and fulfilment everyday
Terrible twos, what have we done?
Cannot turn your back, there are tantrums to come!
Destroying everything, have to think ahead,
Try to juggle it all, would like to go to bed!

We love them so much, although they drive us mad!
If so enjoyable, why when in bed do we feel so glad?
We find children loving and exciting whilst they are awake,
Get them to sleep, time for us we want to make
Most of the time your children you will find by your feet,
With no peace at meal times, interruptions while you eat
You go to the toilet; your privacy has gone,
Seems funny when you need to go, your child needs one
A rare quiet moment, they play or snuggle up to you,
These moments you hold, knowing a child's love is true

Parents

Parents are such strong figures of our upbringing,
When things go wrong, we can find ourselves clinging
Good parents bring us up with love and affection,
Teaching and sending us in the right direction
Unconditional love, they love us no matter what,
Each of us given a start in life, some a little, others a lot
They are here for us when things are good, also when not
so,
Never stop worrying, from us being young to when they
let us go

Children are in a parent's mind, even when we get older,
Always worrying and waiting, in case needed for us to
cry on their shoulder
To children it may come across as nagging, only because
they care,
Becoming a parent one day, you may understand the
worry a parent does bear
For parents we should have utmost respect,
They are just doing their best to protect

Busy Mum

So much going on, so many things to juggle,
Feel you manage it well, sometimes can be a struggle
Mums put themselves under so much pressure; trying to
balance it all,
A job, the house, done enough with the children, the
order is so tall
It is hard not to get tired with such a busy life,
Free time spent with children, you try to be a good wife
Food in the cupboards, clothes to put away,
Always thinking ahead for the next day
Rushed here and there, not much time for yourself,
Second to everyone, even when in bad health
All day you dash around and clock watch, all done with
a smile,
Slap on a bit of make-up, brush hair, and try to keep
some style
Busy all day even when you get home,
Just need a rest, a bit of time alone

Try to be an all-round good mum, sometimes it is hard
and you end up giving in,
Losing patience, feel like what's the point, you are never
going to win
We all have our boundaries; get pushed to our wits end,
We are all human; there is no need to pretend
Find you are repeating yourself over again,
Count to ten so that you don't go insane
You can hear the siblings arguing in the background,
Television, noisy toys, there is always some sound
They come and tell tales, you don't want to know,
You try to smooth things over before you actually blow
It gets to bath time and put the children to bed,
You doze off by their side, your evening wasted ahead

Wake up later and there are still jobs to do,
Put a wash load in, school bags to go through
You know it won't last when you feel yourself get tired
and snappy,
You wake up in the morning, seeing their faces, you are
so happy

Teenager

Growing up, becoming a teenager,
All of a sudden things become major!
Small issues can turn into a drama,
Before becoming a teenager, you felt much calmer

Body changes, you don't like your hair,
It is a task to decide what to wear
Cannot control your feelings, hormones are flying high,
Start to have a crush on someone, randomly start to cry

Always need money; you start to go out,
Want some independence, on your own to get about
Push the boundaries; you have gone too far,
Getting bored, wish you could have a car!
You may sometimes get grounded if in trouble,
You are learning the hard way, head's in a muddle
School is getting harder, when you leave what will you
do?
So many questions and exams to get through

Girls get their monthly cycle; start to wear a bra,
Feeling a little uncomfortable, through many changes
you are
Boys start to shave, a break in their voice,
It just happens they don't get a choice
Start to get extra hair growing in places,
Wear deodorant to cover odours, spots on teenage faces

It isn't always nice going through the changes during
teenage years,
You will soon become an adult, and be over any teenage
tears

Small things in life

Small things in life; stop and think of the small things!
Sight, hearing, sense of smell, to have what each sense
brings
Arms, legs, you have all of your limbs,
See, hear, smell and touch, enjoy daylight until it dims

Feel the sunshine as you walk through a park,
Watch the moon and stars in a sky so dark
Watching loved ones, see children growing up around
you each day,
Enjoy colour, all surroundings, using your eyes to find
your way

Blue sky, sunshine, a white fluffy cloud,
Birds singing, hearing noises, quiet and loud
Fluffy clouds can resemble objects as they take shape,
Moving through a bright blue sky as you drift off, letting
thoughts escape

Hear the joy as children play,
Listen to rain, watch trees sway
Blossom covers grass like a sheet,
The small things, you can feel complete

Feel sand under your feet; listen to the whoosh of the sea,
The smell of cut grass, as you take shade under a tree
Put Wellingtons on, splash in puddles,
Feel clean and relaxed, bathe with bubbles

Joy from music, hymns, pop or rock,
The sound of nothing, sudden deafness would be a shock!
Nice food and drink, cream cakes with cups of tea,
Prefer a can of beer, with your choice of curry
Small things in life, a smile or a hello,
A small thing you do can have a big impact you know!

Feelings

Are you sensitive, or are you hard?
Takes a lot to hurt your feelings, or easily scarred?
Feel for others, emotions run high,
Hear bad news, you easily cry
Find it hard to show how you feel,
You have your own way with problems you deal
Go through a bad patch, brush bad feeling away,
Don't spend time dwelling, move on with a new day

Sometimes think too much, need all of the detail,
Feelings take over, dig too deep, what will unveil?
Keep a level head; keep your feelings in order,
A sensitive balance to stay on the border

Sometimes we get upset, not sure how to feel anymore,
Dig deep down to your feelings, and then you will know
for sure

Shopping

Are you good at buying presents, spending money on
others?
Shopping for close friends and family, sisters and
brothers
You can't enjoy shopping when in a mad rush,
Need to get back, in queues people shove and push
Get home and unpack it all, food shopping isn't great,
Got something for yourself, then you cannot wait!

All different types of shopping, clothes, food or gifts,
Got a lot to do, need to carry a list!
Shopping for yourself, straight away for you it's made,
Are you window shopping until you get paid?
See lots that you like, clothes or shoes,
Can you afford them all, or do you have to choose?
Take a while shopping, what will you buy?
In and out of shops so fast, may depend if a girl or guy!

You cannot decide, you try things on,
Got your size, have you found the right one?
Shopping for something for your home,
Gone to look with friends or need to choose alone?

Shopping can give a buzz, especially if a treat,
Impulse buying, always keep your receipt!

Natalie Mason

Peer pressure

Growing up isn't easy with some peer pressure,
No need to grow up fast, just at your own leisure
In school, joining clubs just want to fit in,
Meet new friends, keep old ones, feels hard to win

Keeping up with the crowd, don't want parents to shout,
Would they approve? Depends what it's about!
Try to make it to days out or a school trip?
Miss out, you feel you're not in with the clique

Keep up with the latest trends,
Have a phone to text your friends
Want new clothes, with a certain name!
Peer pressure what your friends are wearing, you want
to be the same

If only you could see how none of it's a big deal,
All those pressures gone, what a relief you feel!

Days out

Look forward to a good day out,
So many places to get about
Days out with family or just on your own,
A place you have never been or somewhere well known
It could be a park, to take in the view,
Have children with you, is there enough to do?
Go to a fair ground, all ages can enjoy,
Money in the slot machines, win a cuddly toy!
Go for a walk up hills or even mountains,
Can't walk so far, stick to scenery and fountains
Never too old for a day at the zoo,
So many different animals, you can learn something too
Bucket and spade, a picnic at the seaside,
Many beautiful places, your choice is so wide
Take a trip to the swimming baths,
Play with toy floats, have lots of laughs
A day out in the countryside, take in the fresh air,
Have a stroll away from it all, a day without a care
Maybe a few drinks, soaked up with a pub lunch,
A sociable day out with a friendly bunch

We would all like more days out, but have a lot each day to do,
It is nice to have some work or routine, and days out to
look forward to

Nights out

Nights out to relax and to wind down,
A quiet night at the cinema or a night on the town
Down to your local, meet up with friends,
Out with the girls or lads, the occasion depends
Have a few drinks, a gossip and a chat,
On a night out, the world is great from where you're sat
Celebrate a birthday, hen or stag do,
A big occasion, you may try somewhere new
Get dressed up; make an effort to go out,
Laugh, dance and socialise, get some food no doubt
The room may spin if you have too much to drink,
Always seems a good night out, by the morning you may
not think

Bravery

So much will power, although there hangs a dull cloud,
Bravery in life is something of which to be proud
Emotions shared over the years,
Sometimes hidden, others floods of tears

Bravery can be in strength, or helping someone through,
Do your best dealing with such a big issue
Bad times growing up, bullying, abuse, bad childhood,
Still a life to lead, anything to get you through, your
bravery should

Homeless people, they are so brave,
Wish they had a home with money to save,
Living on the streets, hungry and cold,
How brave to face each day, as the reality does unfold

The loss of a partner, you are left on your own,
Maybe left with children, bravery to cope alone
Bravery to get through a loss, a space left inside you,
Especially if it's a child who doesn't reach the age you do

Bravery in saving a life puts you in danger,
Fire fighter as a job or reviving a stranger
Need to tell the truth, need to be brave,
Depending how serious, lives could be saved

Being part of the army, bravery in our troops,
Fighting for our country, bravery in groups
The bravery of watching people die whilst in the army,
Or bravery throughout a natural disaster like a tsunami

People suffer these tragedies, with trauma and fear,
Such bravery moves them forward, why they happen is
not clear

Belief

Many ways for us to believe,
Sometimes up bringing and knowledge we receive
Do you believe in a God, a religion to follow?
Belief can lead to good times, help people through
sorrow
Enjoy visiting church or a holy place?
It is said that God always welcomes a new face
When been to worship God, feel happy and fulfilled,
Feel God carries you through a life you try to build
With Gods help, we are led to do well and to bring peace,
Times may be hard, happiness you will release

Believe in a different world, supernatural, aliens and
U.F.Os,
Read books listen to sightings seen, and your belief just
grows!
Tall thin aliens with big heads and eyes,
Funny green men all different in size?

Life after death, is there another world to go to?
Have to live in this one first and see how we get through
Believe that we come back to this world in re-
incarnation?
Or for you is it all about magic and meditation?
Believe in karma, what goes around comes around?
It may not happen straight away, or a coincidence some
have found

Believe in what you will, so many beliefs and more,
So many questions to ask, we will never know for sure

Breaking up

Breaking up can be devastating, usually if one sided,
You may want the relationship, your partner doesn't
they've decided
Maybe mutual, your relationship just isn't moving on,
Leaves you with a strange empty feeling once your
partner has gone
Spent so much time together, it's getting used to being
alone,
Do you ring or text them, is their number still in your
phone?

Reminders of them everywhere you look,
Music, films, places, foods they would eat or cook
Feeling empty and weak, think about going back,
Try to forget why you broke up, what did the
relationship lack?
There will be special occasions you are invited to,
Times like these you wish you had someone to go with
you

You may think you will never get past this,
There may be times you feel it is them that you miss
Maybe you don't want to settle down; you would rather
stay single,
Wish to explore new places, enjoy being able to mingle

There are always new beginnings as a relationship ends,
You never know who you could meet through family
and friends

Milestones

As we grow up we all hit our milestones,
A lot of parents keep sentiments and memorabilia in
their homes
Hold memories of a first smile,
Caught on camera, pictures taken in a pile
A first curl of hair, a few little locks,
Sometimes parents cut them off to keep in a box

Getting stronger, rolling over and sitting up,
Then you start drinking out of a baby cup
Off the baby food, given solids and start to wean,
You start teething, and then a first tooth is seen
After so long of making sounds you say your first word,
Parents cannot wait to make sure it is heard
As you start to talk more, all listening to what you say,
Hoping it will be 'mummy' or 'daddy' but it's not always
the way

A bit more strength you crawl and climb,
Then you're up and walking in no time
First pair of soled shoes, you get your feet measured,
Some parents keep these in the box with their treasures
Getting clever, eating on your own,
Everybody is saying how much you have grown
You move from a cot to sleeping in a bed over night,
Start using the toilet when you feel the time is right,
First time you remember Santa and the Easter bunny,
Probably remember the presents and chocolate in your
tummy

Been through many milestones, have your first day at
school,
Quite often the first day you cry, parents feel cruel
Tooth goes under your pillow after you start to loose

your milk teeth,
Will the tooth fairy come in and leave something
beneath?
Can write your name with a pen,
Drawing pictures and counting to ten
You ride a bike with stabilisers, the first time on your
own,
When you are bigger they come off and two wheels you
can ride alone
First time you go swimming and swim without aid,
Parents cannot wait to see the progress you have made
A first performance or a school play,
Parents wait to hear lines their child has to say

Start going to high school, it is your first day,
Have to walk, catch a train or bus to get you on your way
Grow into a teenager; get your first boy or girl friend,
Grow into a woman or man, the milestones just don't end
Take driving lessons; maybe get your first car,
Get to an age you are legal to drink, your first time in a
bar
Start your first job; you will remember your first day,
You will always remember the first time you received
your first pay!
One day you may marry and bring up a family of your
own,
The cycle will start all over again as you watch each
milestone

Holidays

Staying in a caravan, camping in a tent,
Sailing on a boat, hotel abroad your holiday is spent
Holiday on a camp site, family and friends, is packed
with fun,
Swimming, beaches, entertainment, can't always get the
sun
It is nice to snuggle up in a warm tent or caravan,
Hear the rain patter on the roof, not bothered about a sun
tan

Spend your holidays on water, a barge on a river with
greenery,
Or with shops, bars, and restaurants on a ship at sea?
Maybe you prefer activities, water sports, golf or ski-ing,
Or carry a map as you visit a place, explore and go sight
seeing

Either keep it simple with your own currency, stick to
what you know,
Or somewhere you haven't been before, enjoy each
holiday where ever you go

Misunderstood

Any single person can be misunderstood,
Don't know where they are coming from, they really
wish you would
We are all so different in personality, and the way we
think,
It can take a while to warm to someone, and to make that
link
They may hold up a guard, it isn't coming down,
You have some good news, they just give a frown

Reasons why people don't open up; inside they may feel
sad,
Sometimes it makes them jealous; they say or do things
bad
Deep down you know they are generous and have a
good heart,
It just needs bringing out of them, the misunderstood
part

A lot of people won't give it time; they have seen one
side,
Need help facing problems that behind they hide
People may be abrupt, sometimes shy,
Others are sensitive, and easily cry

We can all misunderstand each other; take things the
wrong way,
It's not always easy to know the right things to say

School Run

The school run, what a mad time,
Walk, drive or bus, is the weather fine?
Lunch box, P.E. kit, anything else for the school bag?
Last minute letters to read, do mornings make you nag?

Wake yourself up with a walk to school first thing,
Spend time with your children, walk whilst the birds
sing
A walking bus with a few children in a line,
Need to keep the speed up; it can take twice the time
All heading the same way, bump into friends as you
walk,
Friends you already know, or new ones you have a talk

Do you wait at the bus stop; it arrives with the rush of a
crowd,
Want a quiet morning; the school run can be loud
Rainy days slow everything down, seems like all runs
late,
Dodging puddles, wait for the bus, drive to school, no
space at the gate!

A playground of mums stood chattering; another school
run is complete,
The rush is over until pick up time, the children run out
for us to meet

Guidance

We all need a little guidance in our lives some day,
Think we have got a plan, then suddenly loose our way
Some take guidance from good family or friends,
Some pray to God and guidance he sends

Sometimes the loss of a loved one makes you feel like
they are guiding you through,
A guardian angel you feel is there looking down on you
When it all goes wrong we need to be guided back,
Drift off the path for too long, it is guidance that we may
lack

Sometimes our instinct can be a good guide,
Follow your heart, your feeling inside
We all need guidance sometimes when we get it wrong,
Get some guidance; don't waste time as you go along

Natalie Mason

Lucky

Feel so lucky compared to ones who may be close,
Kind of wonder when your luck will end, and may get
your bad dose
Have friends and family, a nice home, even health is
good,
Some people would only wish for one of these if they
could
Hold down a job with enough money, and your
relationship is strong,
Cannot believe you have it all, for some it all goes wrong
Tragic life stories you hear and read,
How lucky you have it with the life that you lead
Someone you know has had a bad time so far,
Try to understand why you are as lucky as you are

It doesn't add up that you are given more, when others
have a lot less,
Wish you could give half of what you have, so they are
out of their mess

46

Decision

Making a decision, how long does it take?
Indecisive, weighing up options or decision fast you make?
Go with your first instinct, make it snappy,
Not sure what is best to keep you happy
Don't think at all, it will be what it will,
Think too deeply, a decision is needed even still
A small decision, if wrong easy to put right,
A big decision, maybe life changing, the future to be bright

Torn two ways in a relationship, job, or moving away,
Pros and cons, if in your mind already, should you stay?
Decisions bring change; you may think it's the wrong choice,
Be positive, give it time, and listen to your own voice
If it doesn't work out and the decision is wrong,
It is just a learning curve which will make you strong

A decision needs to be made, not knowing the outcome until you decide,
You will never know if right or wrong unless you have tried

Sentimental Things

Hold on to a lot of sentimental things
A box thrown in the loft, what memories it brings
Something from your childhood, kept a first teddy bear,
At one time you would carry it everywhere
A special blanket, or something knitted by a family
member,
Look at it all, good times to remember
First time you scribbled a picture or wrote your name,
A christening gown and trinkets, then back in the box
they remain

Sentimental belongings are things we like to treasure,
Hold them close to your heart, they give us much
pleasure

Support

Most of us need some kind of support,
A circle of family and friends, a group of some sort
Living with an addiction, fallen into a bad place,
Generally not coping with life, Cannot keep up with the
pace

A councillor with advice, need someone to talk to,
Support is what you need to get you through
It is good to open up, show how you feel,
Life isn't straight forward; take support to help it heal

Ever received support and wondered what would be if
you didn't get it?
No matter how little or much needed, at a bad time you
hit
Two situations can turn out differently even if start out
the same,
Amounts of pressure and lack of support may be partly
to blame

What a blessing to receive support, looking on it makes
us wise,
We are then able to help others if a time should arise

Lonely

Feeling lonely an emptiness inside,
Don't have close people around you; the gap has grown
too wide
Lost a loved one, your whole life you shared,
For years needed no one else, content and nicely paired

Feeling lonely, starting a life somewhere new?
Moved away with all new places to go to
Sit in your surroundings, no group to hang out,
Need to meet new people to mix with and get about

Feeling lonely want to meet someone new,
Have distance with your real friends who are true
Think you don't need anyone else; all seems well at first,
Don't give up on friends; they are there for you should
the bubble burst

Feeling lonely met mean people, you are feeling shocked,
Suffered from bullying, feel left out, your confidence is
knocked
Feel lonely, struggle to socialize; don't find it easy to mix,
Sometimes a new start, with new people, a lonely life you
can fix

Grief

Everybody may have their own way of handling grief,
Sometimes feel like you won't get over it, other times
may be a relief
A sudden loss is a shock without any warning,
An underlying health problem, you find yourself in
mourning
A loss may be expected for a while, if an illness is the
case,
Carry on day to day, waiting for that phone call each
time and place
Do not want people to suffer, but don't want them to
pass by,
Cannot change their future, all left to do is cry

Lazy Days

Lazy days for most of us rare,
Stay in your pyjamas, don't brush your hair
A day off in the week, others are at work,
Watch day time T.V. it's a real perk
Off for the weekend, watch movies back to back,
Maybe read a book, eat junk food as a snack

Kick back relax, let the mess pile around you,
It will all be there later, with tidying to do
A long bath to soak in with lots of bubbles,
Relax your muscles, take away any troubles

There aren't many days to chill out the whole day
through,
Not done much at all, but feel like a nap is due

Excitement

Excitement, butterflies in your tummy,
Something new, nerves make you come over all funny
Getting ready to go out on a first date,
Those butterflies flutter whilst you wait
Excitement gives energy; your step has a spring,
The wonder and waiting of what it will bring

Going on holiday, excited while you pack your case,
Looking at the brochure, a big smile on your face
Something new in your life, got a cheeky smirk,
Feel happy and lifted even when you are at work

Life can't be exciting all of the way,
You wouldn't feel the same if it were exciting every day

Belong

Feel like you don't belong,
For what ever reason it feels wrong
Adopted or taken into foster care,
Waiting for a new family, you don't know where

Sent to a new home, other children are waiting,
Don't want to get settled; don't want to go on hating
Other children are there to meet, a new room to sleep in,
A family for you? A new life to begin

Sent to many different homes, passed from pillar to post,
Just want to be settled, want a family of your own the
most
Settled into your new home, knowledge of your past you
lack,
A family with brothers or sisters, you may want to know
it all, or never look back!

Christmas

Christmas, such a magical time,
Families join, enjoy mince pies and mulled wine
The run up to Christmas, a few weeks before,
Count down the days, open a calendar door
Write Christmas cards, and a gift list,
Making sure no one is missed
Put up the Christmas tree, decorations and lights,
The streets are bright with all the different types

Going out shopping, hear Christmas music play,
Children perform a nativity, cannot wait to hear what
yours say
Christmas parties start everywhere,
A time for friends and colleges to share
A magical time visiting Santa and his reindeer,
On best behaviour as he asks what children want this
year
He tells them about his elves workshop,
If on the naughty list, the presents will stop!

Have you done everything by Christmas Eve?
A treat for Santa, a carrot for his reindeer we must leave
Put your Christmas stocking out,
On the fire place, or end of bed no doubt
The children are asleep, time to build up toys,
Bringing them out of hiding places, without any noise
He comes from Lapland on Christmas Eve, travelling
whilst reindeer leads his sleigh,
Delivering presents to all good children, around the
world he makes his way

A perfect Christmas morning, open your curtains to a
white layer of snow,

The excitement if Santa has been, the children want to know
Faces light up as they see he has been,
Don't know what to open first, so much they have seen
Maybe a quiet morning, no little feet,
A lie in, breakfast in bed, opening presents is always a treat
Or is your Christmas a busy day?
A rush getting ready with visits to pay

The presents are opened, wrapping paper everywhere,
What a special time for giving and to show you care
The morning goes so fast, almost time for your Christmas meal,
The smell of turkey, the table dressed up gives that Christmas feel
Dinner is served, all tuck in,
Crackers go bang, there are prizes to win
People telling jokes, wearing hats and drinks flowing,
Enjoy the people around you, with the Christmas spirit growing
Time to tidy it all away, so much food goes to waste,
Turkey butties for the next few days, you may get sick of the taste
All full up after eating; now you need a rest,
Flick through the television, you let your food digest
After all of the planning for so many weeks, cannot believe it is here,
Enjoy this festive time we have, and get ready to celebrate the
New Year!

Envy

Envy can be being happy for someone who has a lot,
Although you think it would be nice to have what they
have got
Envy is feeling pleased, they really deserve it,
Envy you are happy and find easy to admit

Maybe you look back at people you thought had it all,
Growing up, centre of attention, there was no shortfall!
Life moves on, reasons for envy may have changed,
Those people may not have what you have now, as life
gets re-arranged

It is easy to feel envious if your life isn't going so well,
Don't let it turn to jealousy; the time will come for your
good spell

Happiness

It's not always straight forward being happy with yourself,
It sounds easy to be happy as long as you have good health
It can take time to like who you are,
Maybe it will happen down life's path quite far

We are made up the same way, just different structure
and size,
Time goes on; we learn to like things we didn't once realise
Try out different hairstyles, define our bodies the best we can,
We all criticise ourselves both woman and man
Try and change parts of you, you have disliked for years,
Everyone has their own style, to mask their own body
fears
Confidence shows through if you are happy on the inside,
Being content with who you are, is always a good guide

We are all equal; let your happiness shine through,
Take all of your positives; the only one who can change it
is you

Dreams

Every night people do dream,
Some remember them, others don't it would seem
We close our eyes and fall asleep,
Our dreams may be light, sometimes deep
Hours of time left to wander is the mind,
Have no control, find your teeth may grind

Strange moments we dream about, things that may
happen in a day,
Dreams tell a story, our subconscious takes over what we
hear and say
There are dreams which may make us sleep talk,
Even wake up in a new room, after a sleep walk
We try to work out dreams which may re-occur,
Movement, crying, words that we slur

We don't always remember dreams when we awake,
Small snippets may come back to us, sense we try to
make
Nightmares, hot sweats, all seem so real,
Wake up in the morning relief we do feel
Nice dreams we wake up and want them to continue,
Try to get back to sleep to see how it ends for you

Try to make sense, do they have a meaning?
We cannot plan our night's sleep, just keep on dreaming
Hope your dreams stay sweet for you,
Each sleep you may dream something new

The Bigger Picture

There is always a bigger picture, try not to be so quick to judge,
Someone may seem rude; reasons behind it, don't hold a grudge
We can be fast to put people down,
They may speak out of tern or give a frown
Look at the bigger picture; it may not be personal to you,
We just don't know the full story of what kind of day they've been through
Their mind filled with worry, have tunnel vision,
Turning it over in their mind, trying to make a decision
How bad would you feel if you gave them a hard time?
Find out later they have had a loss or a victim of crime
Nothing is straight forward; there is always more to it,
To look at the bigger picture, before temper does hit

There has to be a reason for the way someone acts,
Some upset in their life, we don't know the facts!

Natalie Mason

End of an Era

Mixed feelings as you arrive at the end of an Era,
The end of part of your life, but a new path is much
nearer
Growing up, moving out of your family home,
You finish the era of childhood, being free to go alone

Have a long relationship, set in one routine
A sudden change, end of that era, is the grass always green?

As you have a family of your own and settle down,
Miss that era of no responsibility, nights out on the town

As a child leaves nursery to go to school, you may feel
sad,
Get used to the change, more time to yourself, now you
feel glad

End of an era after leaving a job you have worked in for
years,
Not sure what's in front of you, you have certain fears

Maybe moved somewhere new, left an era of life behind,
Excitements of this era, what in life will you find?

The loss of someone, that era you want to hold on to,
Hard to think ahead that you have a new era to get
through

We all go through life as eras come and go,
Some parts more enjoyable, dealing with them as we
grow
Sometimes it can be upsetting reaching the end of an Era,
You move on to the next part of life, after adjustments all
is clearer

Rhymes

Home

Home sweet home,
A place to relax of your own,
Each room reflecting your taste,
Furniture and possessions strategically placed
Our homes are unique with their own colour scheme,
Some calm and bland, others bright colours they ream
For some it is a social place, friends come in and out,
A warm welcome, a party home for gatherings it's all about
On days off we work on our homes, make them comfortable in our own way,
Maybe come home to shut off from the world after a hard day

Guilt

Ever done something wrong?
Tried to hold a secret for too long?
Your conscience has got to you, you are feeling bad,
Wishing you hadn't, it is making you feel sad
You can move forward and live each day,
Do the right thing, guilt doesn't easily go away

Ambition

Strive for ambition, want to go far,
See yourself being famous, even a pop star
No matter what you do, you are on a mission,
Work hard and do well to reach your ambition
Motivation, discipline, plan where you want to be,
Don't stop until you're there, results you want to see
Succeed with your ambition, become addicted to the
adrenaline rush,
Like the feeling of success, ambition to go further gives
you that push!

Exams

Setting your books up ready to revise,
Fed up before you start, getting heavy eyes
Have got your own way to remember?
Read, write, or listen, it will all be over by September
Revise for a minute, feels like an hour,
So many snack breaks, you need brain power
You are getting closer to an exam,
Learnt enough, or about to cram?
The funny tummy nerves are running high,
Can't do anymore, your best you can only try

Natalie Mason

Bad Hair Day

Bad hair day,
What can I say!
Long, short, thick or thin,
Bad hair day, you cannot win

In a style curly or straight hair,
Bad hair day, you cannot bare
Colour, highlights in bad condition,
Need a change, you are on a mission

Flick through the mags for a new look,
It's a hairdresser's appointment you need to book!

Alcohol

Can be fun or sometimes not,
Is yours a long drink or a shot?
Wake up with a sore head in the morning,
Feel it should have come with a warning!
Some people can handle alcohol; others it makes them change,
Becoming funny and more loving, emotional, angry or strange
Have fun, wind down, laugh and relax,
Too much can make you moody, analysing life's facts

House Work

House work, it needs doing again!
Who messed up this time, who can I blame?
So much to do, hoover and dust,
Some don't bother, some feel they must
Spending hours cleaning, scrubbing the grime,
Wouldn't mind so much if it lasted any time
The house work will always be there tomorrow, and will
be back again,
If offered something better to do, don't let the cleaning
drive you insane!

Manners

Manners, they really cost nothing,
People do forget them, arrogant or rushing?
Manners are a big deal; they can help get you a long way,
'Many thanks, please, thank you, ta, cheers,' all different
ways we can say

New job

Looking for a new job, didn't have one anyway?
Bored of the old one, just want more pay!
Plodding on each day, there has to be something better,
Applying for lots of jobs, waiting for that letter
A new job starting today,
Feeling nervous on the way
First days always hard, have you done the right thing?
Enjoy your new challenge, see what it will bring

Money

Money makes the world go around,
Do you have a lot or just a few pounds?
Quite well off, buy what ever you please,
Can only window shop, wish money grew on trees
Easy to put on a credit card,
Paying it off is the bit that's hard
Come into money, feels great, so many things to spend it
on,
Think carefully, don't waste it, once it's there and then
it's gone!
Work hard to earn money, spend what you can afford,
If money grew on trees, you would only get bored!

Pets

Lots of us have pets, popular ones are dogs and cats,
Some of us like to keep rodents, such as hamsters, mice
or rats
Easily attached to pets, they become a family member,
Train them from a young age; it's amazing what they
remember
Take dogs for walks, cats will roam,
Love and talk to pets, they become a part of your home
Pets given love will give love back,
Just like some humans, if not treated well, they may
attack
Not forgetting pets can be expensive to keep,
Food, vets' fees, saw dust and bedding, they don't
always come cheap

Clutter and Junk

Are you surrounded with clutter and junk?
Your space around you has rapidly shrunk
Clear out the items you do not use,
When out buying new, be careful what you choose
Sometimes it is hard to clear things out,
If you haven't used it in a while, have no doubt
A good de clutter can make you feel good,
Could have done it a long time ago if you knew it would

Natalie Mason

Surprise

The waiting, the wonder of a surprise,
It gets to the moment you can't believe your eyes
Small, big or something to do,
The excitement of guessing, you are given a clue
You know where the surprise is, come across it as you
sneak,
Can you hold back and wait, are you tempted to peak?
It is nice to know somebody has surprised and given you
a thought,
It is best when it's something you want, but wouldn't
have ever bought

Around the Corner

What's around the corner, we never know what's there?
One moment it's all going wrong, the next we don't have
a care
Going through the highs and lows,
Mixed emotions, explosive blows
Enjoy the good times as long as they last,
Deal with the bad times and put them in the past
Good or bad times, can't always last forever,
Love the good, come through the bad, just keep your
head together

Natalie Mason

Exercise

We should all do some exercise,
Make our heart rate pump and rise
Helps to keep the weight off us,
Live a healthy life style so it does
Some of us love it, and get addicted,
Others cannot stand it, do none or are restricted
Have a run, go to the gym,
Keep fit classes to keep us slim
Hate the thought of exercise, no motivation,
Never miss a work out, go without hesitation
Feel great when you've had a work-out, released those
endorphins,
Glad you have done it, got bags of energy and feel full of
beans!

Friends

True friends or just an acquaintance?
Always there for you or just high maintenance?
Boyfriend or girlfriend or just a best friend,
Can relax, confide, have trust, or feels pretend?
Have been friends for years,
Have seen laughs and tears
Pamper and shopping days,
Best friends in lots of ways

Natalie Mason

Sleep

Sleep, rest, catnap or have Zzzzz's,
We all get tired and need our beds
Love having sleep, need eight hours a night?
Go to bed early, don't wake up till light!
Head hits the pillow, asleep straight away,
Can relax, close your eyes after a busy day
Don't need many hours, manage on just a few,
Stay up reading, watching tele, up until two
That nice cosy bed, all warm inside,
Sleep all cuddled up in a ball, or arms and legs out wide?
Busy lives, don't get much sleep,
Just a light sleeper, cannot drift off too deep
Not getting your sleep can leave you feeling rough,
We all need our beauty sleep; it shows if not had enough

Sweet dreams, enjoy your next sleep ahead,
Recipe for being tired, your own comfy bed!

Tributes

Angel

An Angel on this earth or from heaven above,
We know you are an Angel with the way you carry love
Have a lot to deal with, others always come first,
Never show you are feeling low, an oar of happiness you
burst
How do you do it, the burden you take on?
You must be an Angel, no doubt in my mind you are one
Here to listen, give time to talk,
Follow in Angel footsteps you do walk

Angels don't ask for anything in return,
They are happy to give, just hope Angel ways we learn
Lots of patience, always stays calm,
Juggle so much, keeping up a charm
Finding the best in others, a chance to trust and give,
Do it without thinking, an Angel is how you live
Always a reason why people seem grumpy or sad,
Angel understands instead of marking them as bad

Others look on and want to be more like you,
Oh what an Angel through and through
When feeling down the Angel is there,
See them or not, you feel a lift as they care

Dedicated to my mum, an Angel I have always said,
Believe she has been sent to earth to guide as many as
she can ahead
An Angel I have always known,
Given me Angel guidance as I have grown

One day she may not be here, at least not for me to see,
I will try to keep up her Angel ways, like her I wish to be.

Sarah

Sarah lost her life at the age of sixteen,
Such a young girl, a short life feels so mean
Always so popular, made up games in the playground,
Had a great bedroom, and toys, sleepovers with friends
around
A sleepover with a big feast, and a late night,
Crisps for breakfast, no idea that life would be a fight

Dogs, rabbits, hamsters, her pets she had love for,
Anything to do with pigs, she carried on collecting more
Halloween she loved to dress up, scary movies she was
into,
Such quirkiness about her, always exciting and new
Memories of being at the caravan, or school holidays,
with Nana and Granddad,
Growing up, then into hair and makeup, shopping and
fun we had

We went to different high schools, both our separate ways,
Made new friends, thought nothing of it, growing
through school days
Now and again our mums saw each other; we heard that
Sarah was ill,
Her appearance had charged with steroids, it didn't
register how serious still
She couldn't complete her exams at school in her last year,
That sounded good to us, being young and naïve, at least
we are still here!

For us we couldn't wait to finish, thinking of our future
ahead,
College, jobs, starting families, our lives starting, Sarah's
ending instead

Her funeral was packed out with friends, amazing for a
life not so long,
Words spoken highly and remembrance given in her
favourite types of song

A couple of years later I had a daughter of my own,
surprisingly on Sarah's birthday,
My Rebecca makes me proud, and reminds me of Sarah
in a way

1993

Natalie Mason

Denise

Just a few words for a very brave lady,
That is for sure and not just maybe

It won't be easy whilst you are sleeping,
From us there will be a lot of weeping

Don't you worry; we will be by your side,
Waiting for your eyes to open wide

You have lots of family and friends too,
Mates from the Grapes, like Brian and Sue

Plenty of others thinking of you there,
It won't be long before you are back doing hair

Don't worry about your husband Dave,
We will all make sure he does behave
Lee will keep him busy and take him out,
He will look after him there's no doubt

As for Glenda, Jessica, and Steve,
They will look after each other, I do believe

The kids will miss you as they are always looked after,
With more then enough toys, chocolate and laughter

We know you look forward to being out,
Back to yourself, buzzing about

Denise Mason – Pre operation 2004

Granddad Harry

Granddad Harry, you know you will be missed,
So many reasons I have a long list
You would wake up early everyday,
Singing and happy in every way

Young and old, everyone got on with you,
All of my friends thought you were cool
You would have a laugh and a drink in the pub,
Even known to go to a club

Snooker was the thing you really enjoyed,
All of the times you lost, you never got annoyed
Friends will miss you, who you played in the club,
Maybe you will get a chance to win from above

Family days out, no more waiting for the bathroom,
That was just you being so well groomed
You would always have a new joke to tell,
A silly rhyme you would tell them well

You are loved so much, your wife Iris will be sad,
Your loving children, Denise, Gary and John will miss
you as their dad
Not just a Granddad, a great one too,
We are grateful of the years we have had with you

I put a few words together today,
I get from you I am proud to say
You loved the Tina Turner song
"You are Simply the Best"
We will play it for you as we put you to rest!

Read at Funeral - 19.5.2004

Nanna Iris

Nanna Iris we already miss you,
A happy life, looking after other's on your way through

When she was well she loved to sew,
Her talents were endless with decorating, gardening and
D.I.Y. you know

She loved her caravans all of her life,
Once again shared them, working hard to keep them nice

On days out it was to charity shops or a car boot,
Oh she did love to have a good root

She loved her family and friends as we all know,
Her great grand children certainly gave her a glow
She loved it when Rebecca told her jokes,
Usually being cheeky about the old folks

Kayleigh caught on that Nanna was slow on her feet,
She would run up and pinch a biscuit or sweet
There was always a nice stock by Nanna's side,
Kayleigh would run up, take one, and then hide

It is her little ways we shall all miss,
A cup of tea, her T.V. soaps, she was in total bliss
We all knew to be quiet whilst she was watching the
soaps,
There was no way anyone got near those remotes
For someone who was short of sight and a little deaf,
Nanna Iris always knew which buttons to press

We thank God for letting us have you for all of these
years,

Though it is now time for us to shed our tears
Good night, God Bless Nanna, enjoy your rest,
We know you are with Granddad now, you were both…
"Simply the Best!"

Read at funeral – 4.7.2010

Lightning Source UK Ltd.
Milton Keynes UK
UKOW040224061212

203253UK00001B/11/P